MY MANY-COATED MAN

LAURIE LEE

My Many=coated Man

1961
WILLIAM MORROW AND COMPANY, INC.
NEW YORK

PRINTED IN THE NETHERLANDS BY DRUKKERIJ HOLLAND N.V., AMSTERDAM

TO
W. G.

NOTE

This selection has been made only from poems written since the war, and my grateful acknowledgements are due to the Editors of *The Listener*, *Orpheus*, *Penguin New Writing*, *Punch* and *The New Yorker*, in whose pages they first appeared.

L. L.

CONTENTS

BOY IN ICE

O river, green and still,
By frost and memory stayed,
Your dumb and stiffened glass divides
A shadow and a shade.

In air, the shadow's face
My winter gaze lets fall
To see beneath the stream's bright bars
That other shade in thrall.

A boy, time-fixed in ice,
His cheeks with summer dyed,
His mouth, a rose-devouring rose,
His bird-throat petrified.

O fabulous and lost,
More distant to me now
Than rock-drawn mammoth, painted stag
Or tigers in the snow.

You stare into my face
Dead as ten thousand years,
Your sparrow tongue sealed in my mouth
Your world about my ears.

And till our shadows meet,
Till time burns through the ice,
Thus frozen shall we ever stay
Locked in this paradise.

I

BOMBAY ARRIVAL

Slow-hooved across the carrion sea,
Smeared by the betel-spitting sun,
Like cows the Bombay islands come
Dragging the mainland into view.

The loose flank loops the rocky bone,
The light beats thin on horn and hill;
Still breeds the flesh for hawks, and still
The Hindu heart drips on a stone.

Around the wide dawn-ridden bay
The waters move their daggered wings;
The dhow upon its shadow clings—
A dark moth pinioned to the day.

False in the morning, screened with silk,
Neat as an egg the Town draws near,
False as a map her streets appear
Ambling, and odourless as milk.

Until she holds us face to face—
A crumbling mask with bullet pores,
A nakedness of jewels and sores
Clutched with or guilt in her embrace.

THE EDGE OF DAY

The dawn's precise pronouncement waits
With breath of light indrawn,
Then forms with smoky, smut-red lips
The great O of the sun.

The mouldering atoms of the dark
Blaze into morning air;
The birdlike stars droop down and die,
The starlike birds catch fire.

The thrush's tinder throat strikes up,
The sparrow chips hot sparks
From flinty tongue, and all the sky
Showers with electric larks.

And my huge eye a chaos is
Where molten worlds are born;
Where floats the eagle's flaming moon,
And crows, like clinkers, burn;

Where blackbirds scream with comet tails,
And flaring finches fall,
And starlings, aimed like meteors,
Bounce from the garden wall;

Where, from the edge of day I spring
Alive for mortal flight,
Lit by the heart's exploding sun
Bursting from night to night.

TWELFTH NIGHT

No night could be darker than this night,
no cold so cold,
as the blood snaps like a wire,
and the heart's sap stills,
and the year seems defeated.

O never again, it seems, can green things run,
or sky birds fly,
or the grass exhale its humming breath
powdered with pimpernels,
from this dark lung of winter.

Yet here are lessons for the final mile
of pilgrim kings;
the mile still left when all have reached
their tether's end: that mile
where the Child lies hid.

For see, beneath the hand, the earth already
warms and glows;
for men with shepherd's eyes there are
signs in the dark, the turning stars,
the lamb's returning time.

Out of this utter death he's born again,
his birth our saviour;
from terror's equinox he climbs and grows,
drawing his finger's light across our blood—
the sun of heaven, and the son of god.

THE EASTER GREEN

Not dross, but dressed with good,
Is this gold air;
Not bald nor bare
But bearded like a god
Grown old more fair.

Dazed from the pit I see
Glazes of holy light
On day and diamond night;
Through every sun I hear
The chiming aconite.

By husk and darkness fed
My appetite grows keen,
By buried lusts made lean
Child-tongued I suck sweet bread
And kiss the virgin green.

I, from the well new-drawn,
With root and flower am crowned—
Drowsed, but not drowned.
The Easter-father blesses with a lamb;
The son is not disowned.

So shall I know, come fall,
Come flesh returning frail,
This shriving shall not fail:
The green blood flushing at the heart
Anoints the prodigal.

MY MANY-COATED MAN

Under the scarlet-licking leaves,
through bloody thought and bubbly shade,
the padded, spicy tiger moves—
a sheath of swords, a hooded blade.

The turtle on the naked sand
peels to the air his pewter snout
and rubs the sky with slotted shell—
the heart's dismay turned inside out.

The rank red fox goes forth at night
to bite the gosling's downy throat,
then digs his grave with panic claws
to share oblivion with the stoat.

The mottled moth, pinned to a tree,
woos with his wings the bark's disease
and strikes a fungoid, fevered pose
to live forgotten and at ease.

Like these, my many-coated man
shields his hot hunger from the wind,
and, hooded by a smile, commits
his private murder in the mind.

SUNKEN EVENING

The green light floods the city square—
  A sea of fowl and feathered fish,
  Where squalls of rainbirds dive and splash
And gusty sparrows chop the air.

Submerged, the prawn-blue pigeons feed
  In sandy grottoes round the Mall,
  And crusted lobster-buses crawl
Among the fountains' silver weed.

There, like a wreck, with mast and bell,
  The torn church settles by the bow,
  While phosphorescent starlings stow
Their mussel shells along the hull.

The oyster-poet, drowned but dry,
  Rolls a black pearl between his bones;
  The typist, trapped by telephones,
Gazes in bubbles at the sky.

Till, with the dark, the shallows run,
  And homeward surges tide and fret—
  The slow night trawls its heavy net
And hauls the clerk to Surbiton.

SONG BY THE SEA

Girl of green waters, liquid as lies,
Cool as the calloused snow,
From my attic brain and prisoned eyes
Draw me and drown me now.

O suck me down to your weeds and fates,
Green horizontal girl,
And in your salt-bright body breed
My death's dream-centred pearl.

For locked alive in the brutal bone
I feel my lust of love
Rolling her porpoise thighs alone
Where the tropic channels move.

Her smooth mouth moons among the tides
Sipping the milky fishes,
Her fallow, shallow breasts pile up
Tight with my secret wishes.

Girl of green waters, liquid as light,
Beneath your skin of suns
My frights and frenzies moan asleep,
My deeds are skeletons.

So suck me down to your bed of sand,
Dilute my serpent blood,
Then lift the stain from my crimson hand
And sink it in your flood.

TO MATTHEW SMITH

Fused with the minerals of sun and earth,
spurting with smoke of flowers,
oil is incendiary on your moving brush;
your hands are jets
that crack the landscape's clinker and draw forth
its buried incandescence.

These molten moments brazed in field and flesh
burn out for us,
but you can stand and nail within a frame
the fire we mourn,
can catch the pitchpine hour and keep its flame
pinned at the point of heat.

Our summer's noon you pour into a mould,
a rose its furnace;
through green and blue its burning seeds unfold,
through night and day:
raked by your eyes the paint has never cooled.

SCOT IN THE DESERT

All day the sand, like golden chains,
The desert distance binds;
All day the crouching camels groan,
Whipped by the gritty winds.

The mountain, flayed by sun, reveals
Red muscles, wounds of stone,
While on its face the black goats swarm
And bite it to the bone.

Here light is death; on every rock
It stretches like a cry,
Its fever burns up every bush,
It drinks each river dry.

It cracks with thirst the creviced lip,
It fattens black the tongue,
It turns the storm cloud into dust,
The morning dew to dung.

Men were not made to flourish here,
They shroud their heads and fly—
Save one, who stares into the sun
With sky-blue British eye.

Who stares into the zenith sun
And smiles and feels no pain,
Blood-cooled by Calvin, mist and bog,
And summers in the rain.

LONG SUMMER

Gold as an infant's humming dream,
Stamped with its timeless, tropic blush,
The steady sun stands in the air
And burns like Moses' holy bush.

And burns while nothing it consumes;
The smoking branch but greener grows,
The crackling briar, from budded lips,
A floating stream of blossom blows.

A daze of hours, a blaze of noons,
Licks my cold shadow from the ground;
A flaming trident rears each dawn
To stir the blood of earth around.

Unsinged beneath the furnace sky
The frenzied beetle runs reborn,
The ant his antic mountain moves,
The rampant ram rewinds his horn.

I see the crazy bees drop fat
From tulips ten times gorged and dry;
I see the sated swallow plunge
To drink the dazzled waterfly.

A halo flares around my head,
A sunflower flares across the sun,
While down the summer's seamless haze
Such feasts of milk and honey run

That lying with my orchid love,
Whose kiss no frost of age can sever,
I cannot doubt the cold is dead,
The gold earth turned to good—forever.

APPLES

Behold the apples' rounded worlds:
juice-green of July rain,
the black polestar of flower, the rind
mapped with its crimson stain.

The russet, crab and cottage red
burn to the sun's hot brass,
then drop like sweat from every branch
and bubble in the grass.

They lie as wanton as they fall,
and where they fall and break,
the stallion clamps his crunching jaws,
the starling stabs his beak.

In each plump gourd the cidery bite
of boys' teeth tears the skin;
the waltzing wasp consumes his share,
the bent worm enters in.

I, with as easy hunger, take
entire my season's dole;
welcome the ripe, the sweet, the sour,
the hollow and the whole.

HOME FROM ABROAD

Far-fetched with tales of other worlds and ways,
My skin well-oiled with wines of the Levant,
I set my face into a filial smile
To greet the pale, domestic kiss of Kent.

But shall I never learn? That gawky girl,
Recalled so primly in my foreign thoughts,
Becomes again the green-haired queen of love
Whose wanton form dilates as it delights.

Her rolling tidal landscape floods the eye
And drowns Chianti in a dusky stream;
The flower-flecked grasses swim with simple horses,
The hedges choke with roses fat as cream.

So do I breathe the hayblown airs of home,
And watch the sea-green elms drip birds and shadows,
And as the twilight nets the plunging sun
My heart's keel slides to rest among the meadows.

TOWN OWL

On eves of cold, when slow coal fires,
rooted in basements, burn and branch,
brushing with smoke the city air;

When quartered moons pale in the sky,
and neons glow along the dark
like deadly nightshade on a briar;

Above the muffled traffic then
I hear the owl, and at his note
I shudder in my private chair.

For like an augur he has come
to roost among our crumbling walls,
his blooded talons sheathed in fur.

Some secret lure of time it seems
has called him from his country wastes
to hunt a newer wasteland here.

And where the candalabra swung,
bright with the dancers' thousand eyes,
now his black, hooded pupils stare,

And where the silk-shoed lovers ran
with dust of diamonds in their hair,
he opens now his silent wing,

And, like a stroke of doom, drops down,
and swoops across the empty hall,
and plucks a quick mouse off the stair . . .

THE ABANDONED SHADE

Walking the abandoned shade
of childhood's habitations,
my ears remembering chime,
hearing their buried voices.

Hearing original summer,
the birdlit banks of dawn,
the yellow-hammer beat of blood
gilding my cradle eyes.

Hearing the tin-moon rise
and the sunset's penny fall,
the creep of frost and weep of thaw
and bells of winter robins.

Hearing again the talking house
and the four vowels of the wind,
and midnight monsters whispering
in the white throat of my room.

Season and landscape's liturgy,
badger and sneeze of rain,
the bleat of bats, and bounce of rabbits
bubbling under the hill:

Each old and echo-salted tongue
sings to my backward glance;
but the voice of the boy, the boy I seek,
within my mouth is dumb.